This
Notebook
belongs to

Handwriting Practice A-Z

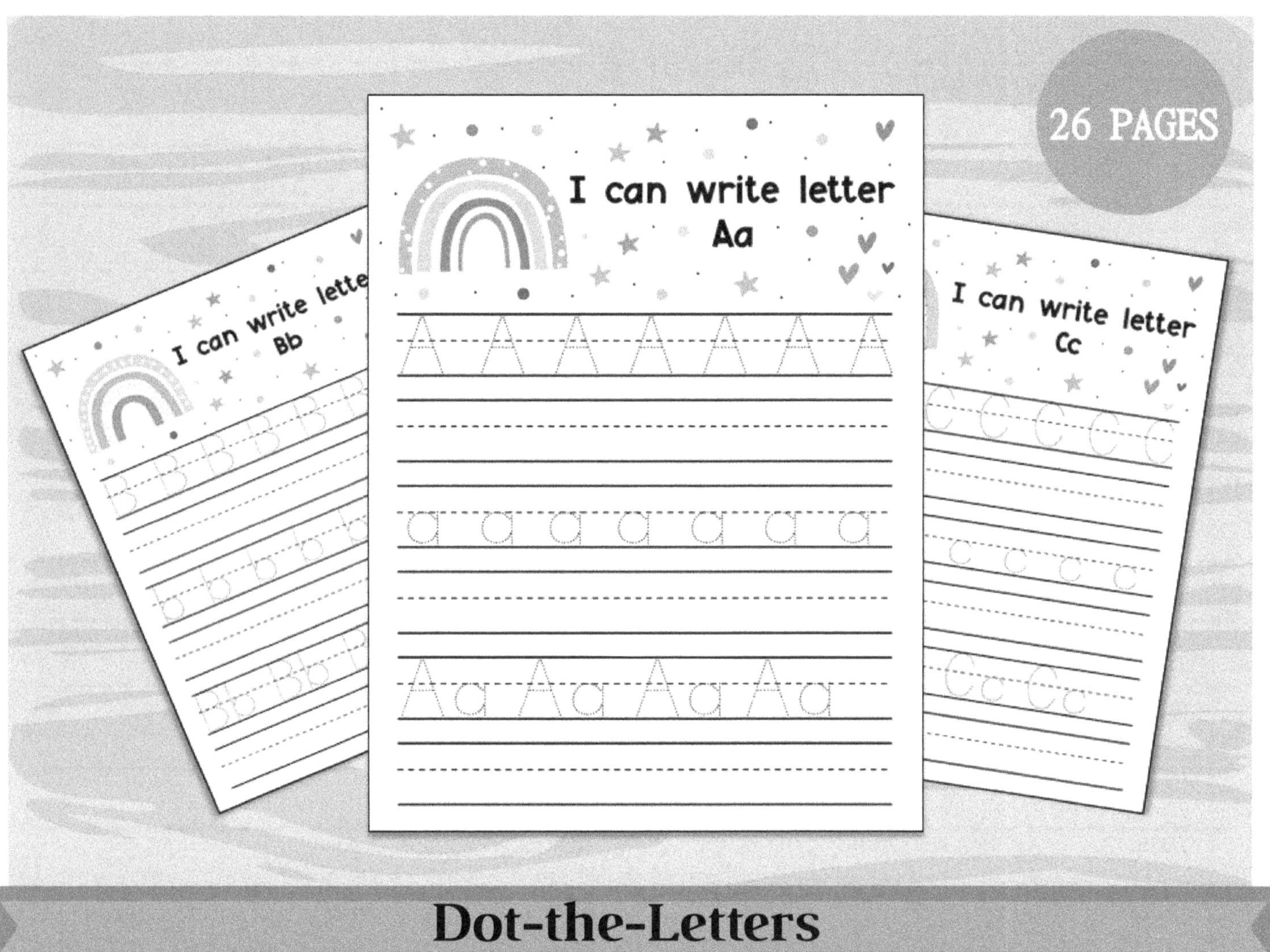

Dot-the-Letters

Daytona Thorson

I can write letter Aa

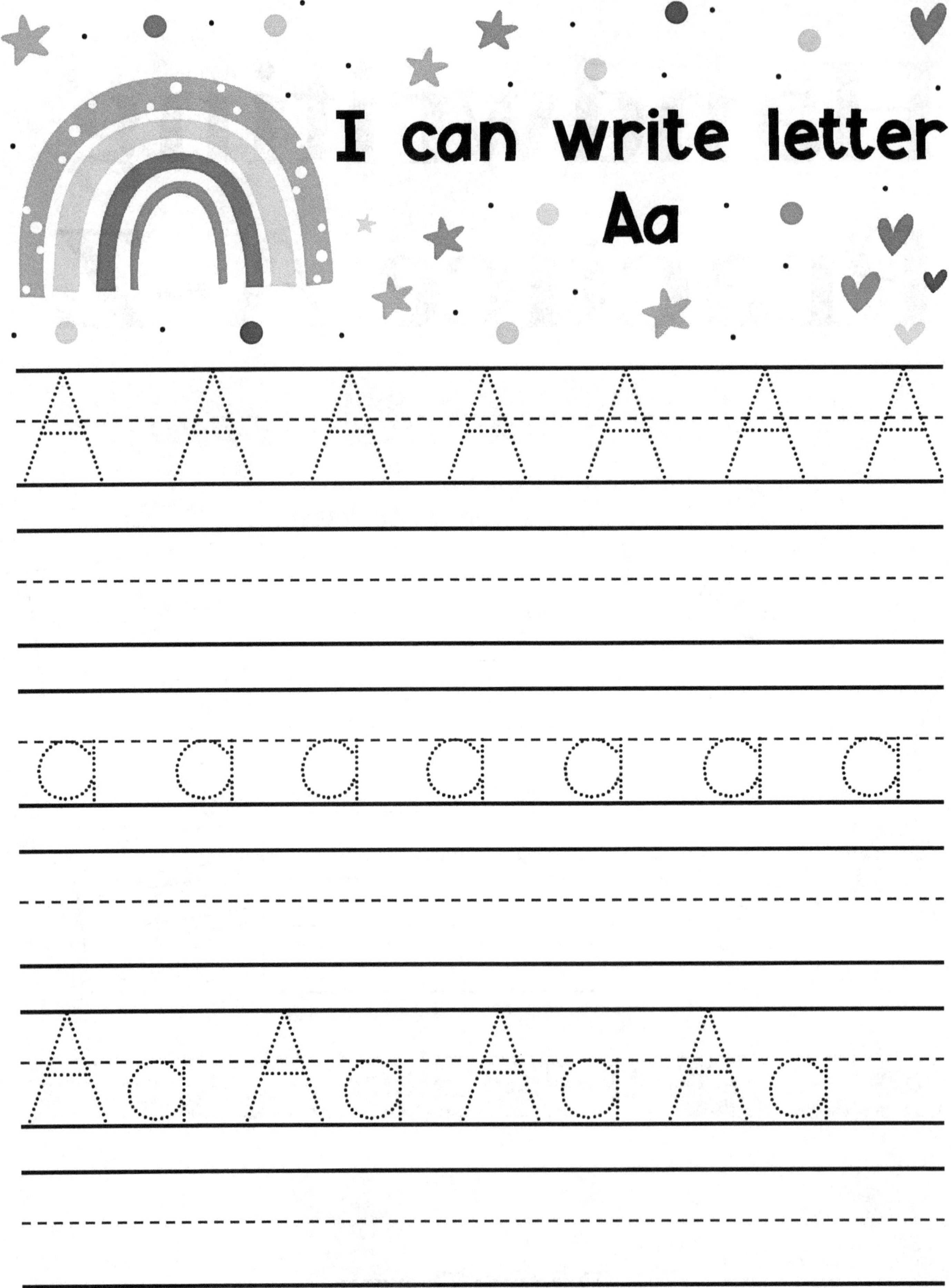

I can write letter Bb

I can write letter
Cc

I can write letter Dd

I can write letter Ee

I can write letter Ff

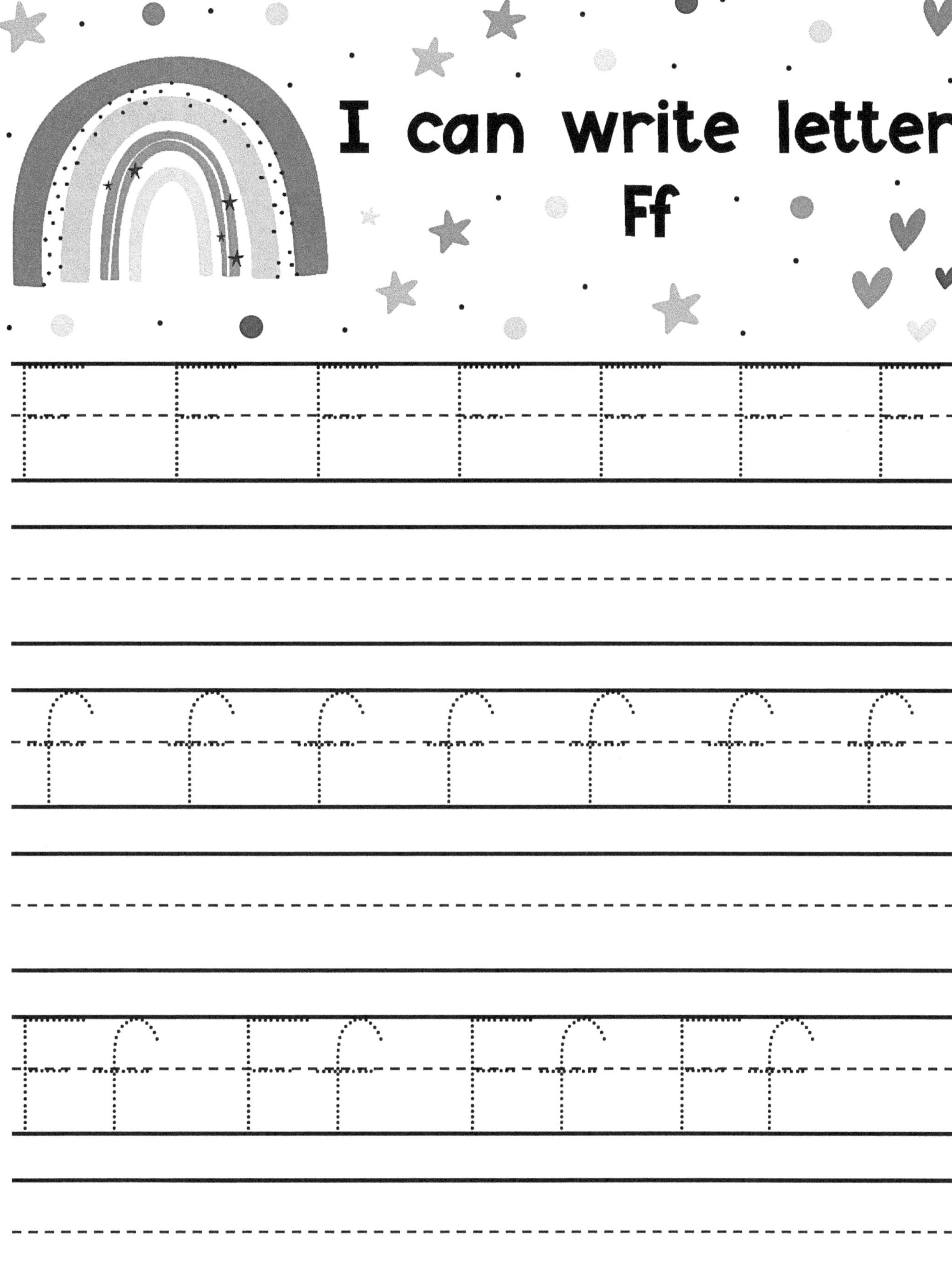

I can write letter Gg

I can write letter Hh

I can write letter Ii

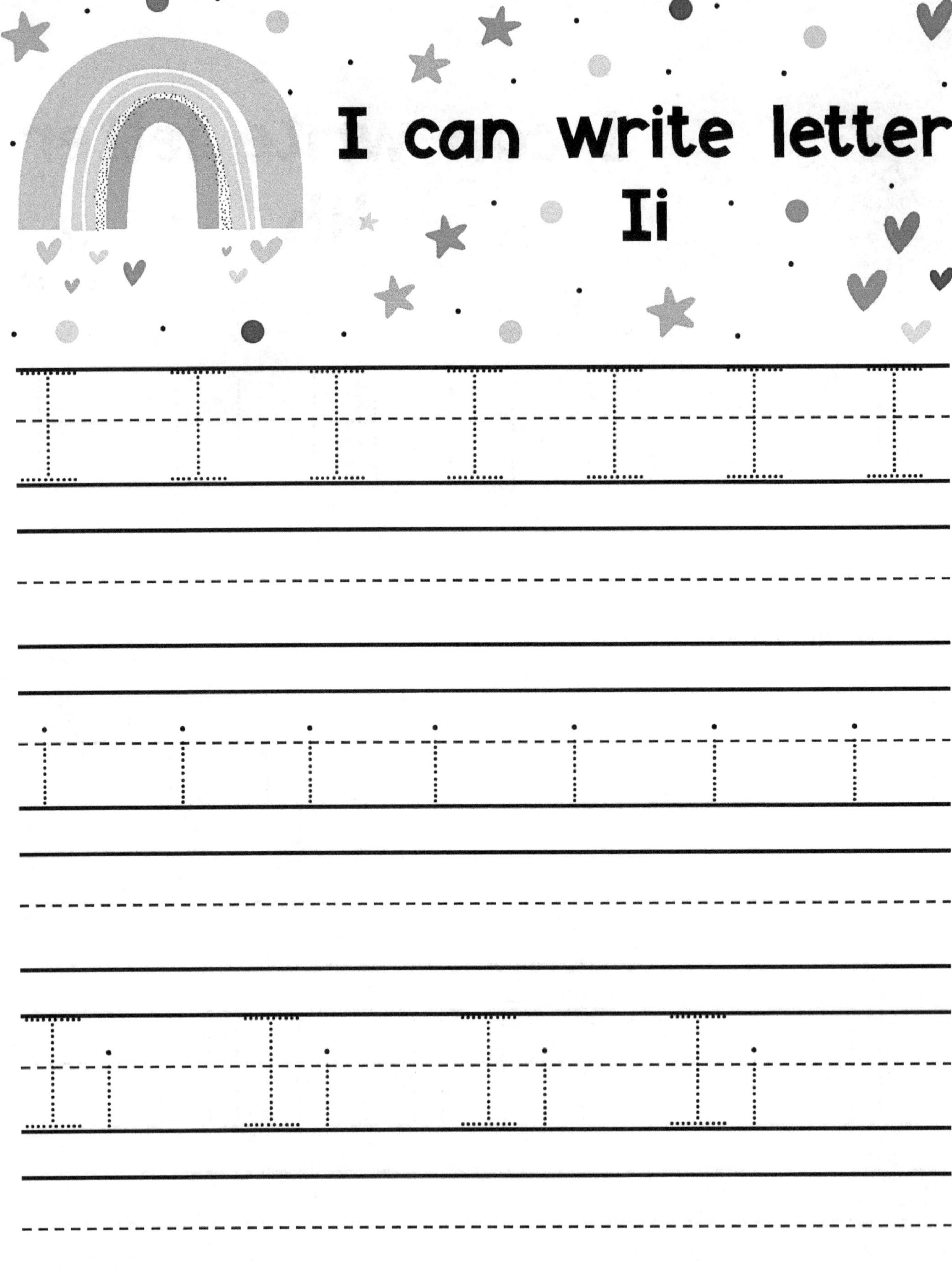

I can write letter Jj

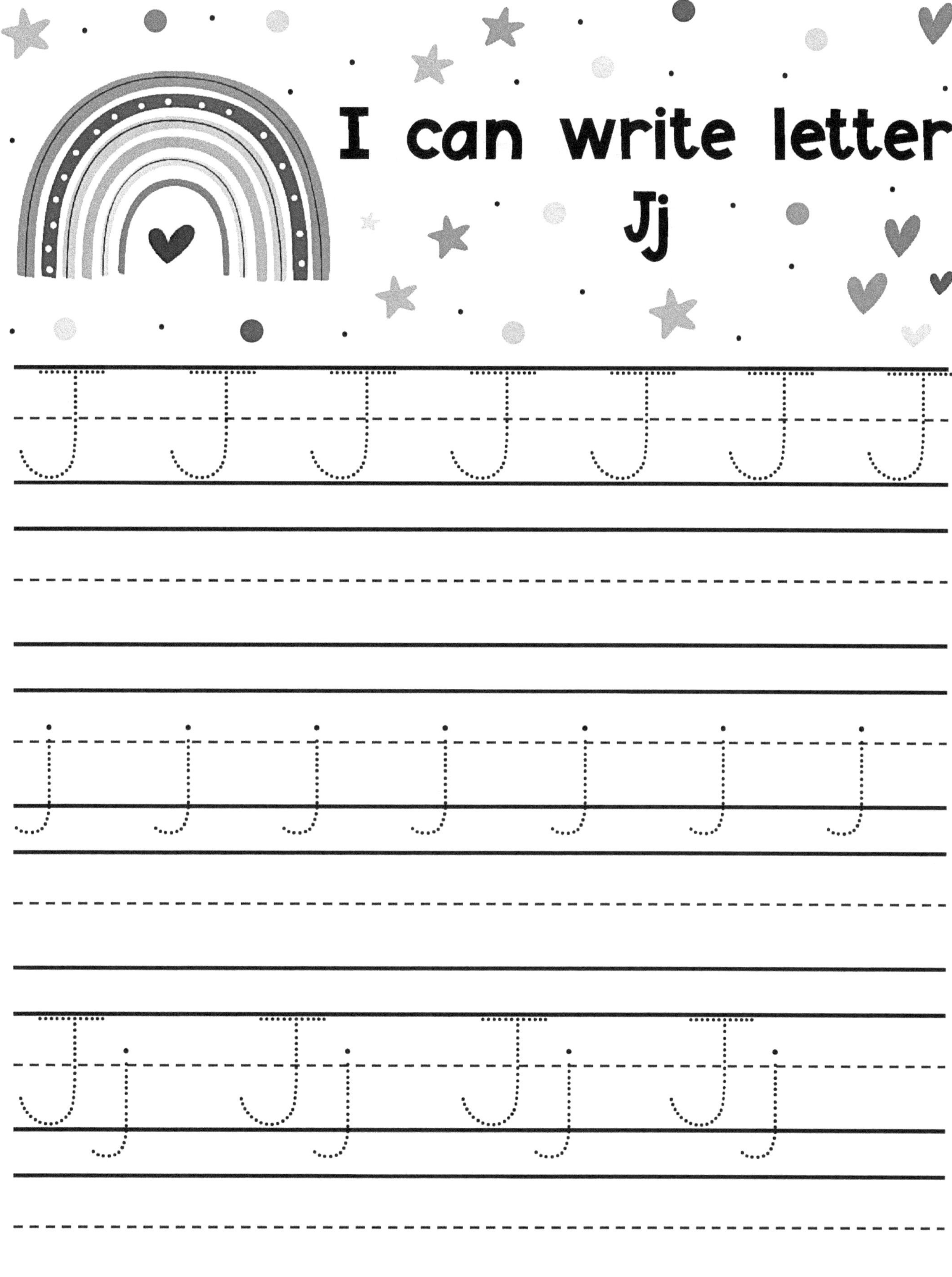

I can write letter Kk

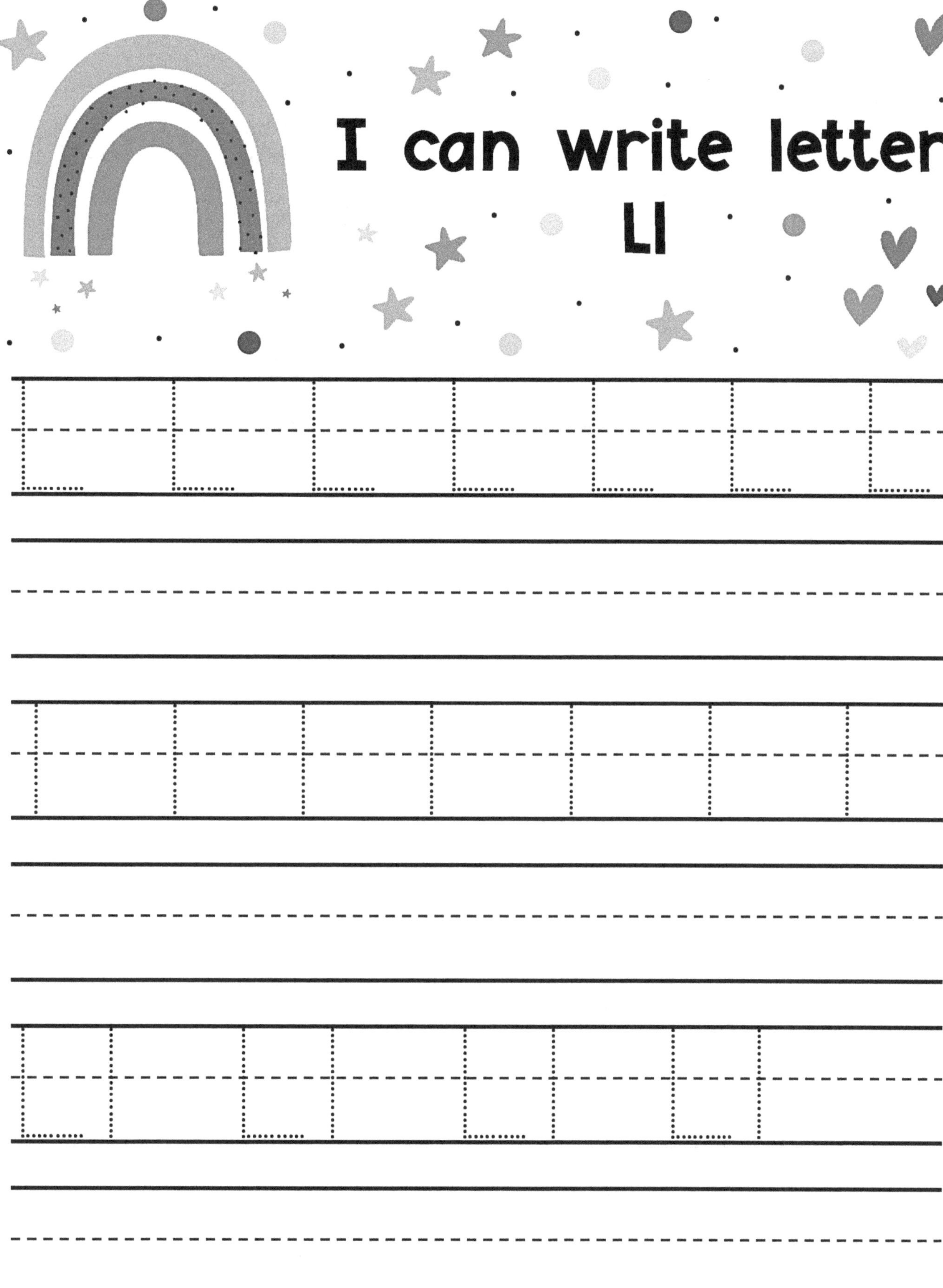

I can write letter
Ll

I can write letter Mm

I can write letter Nn

I can write letter Oo

I can write letter Pp

I can write letter Qq

I can write letter Rr

I can write letter Ss

I can write letter Tt

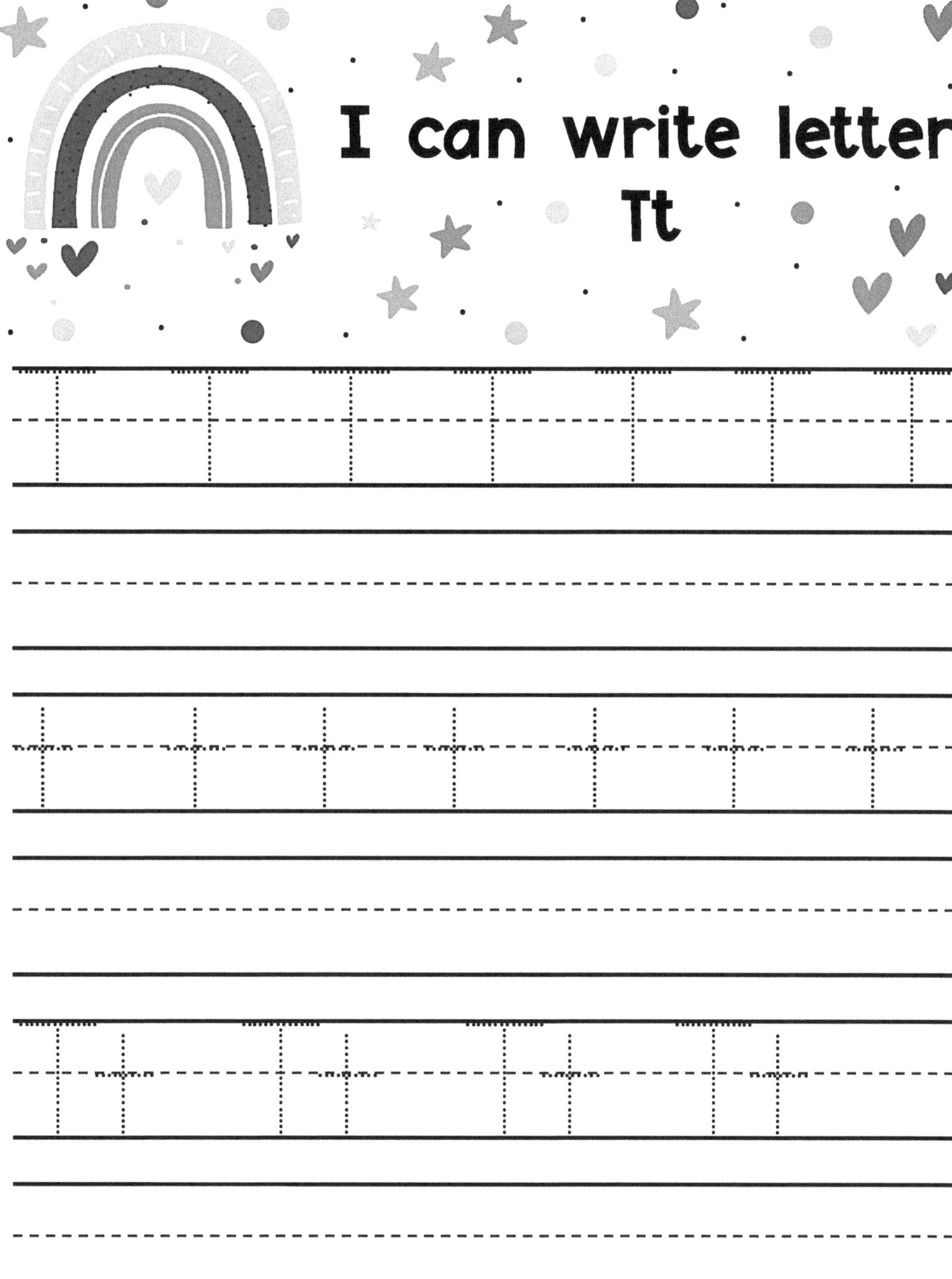

I can write letter Uu

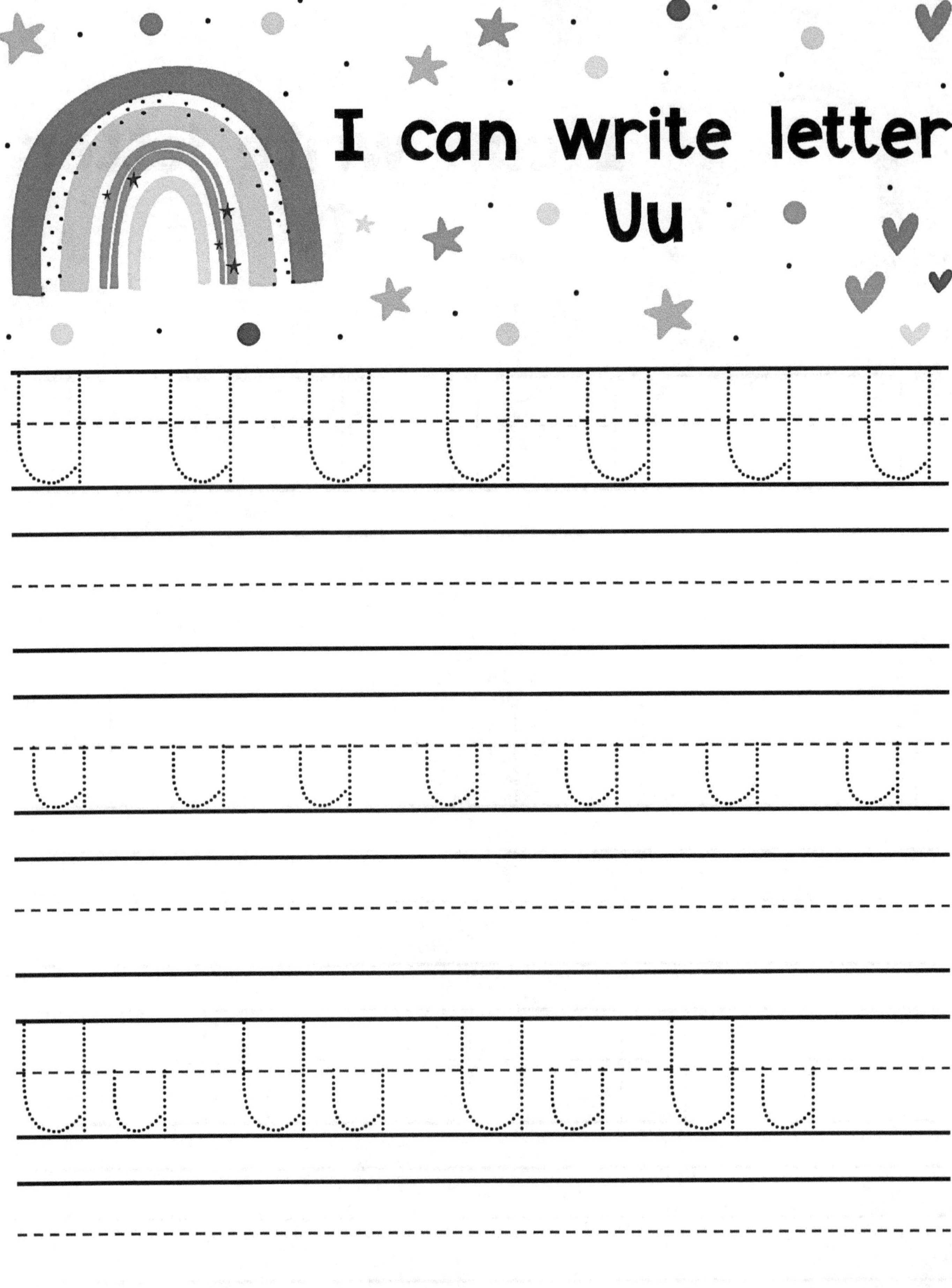

I can write letter Vv

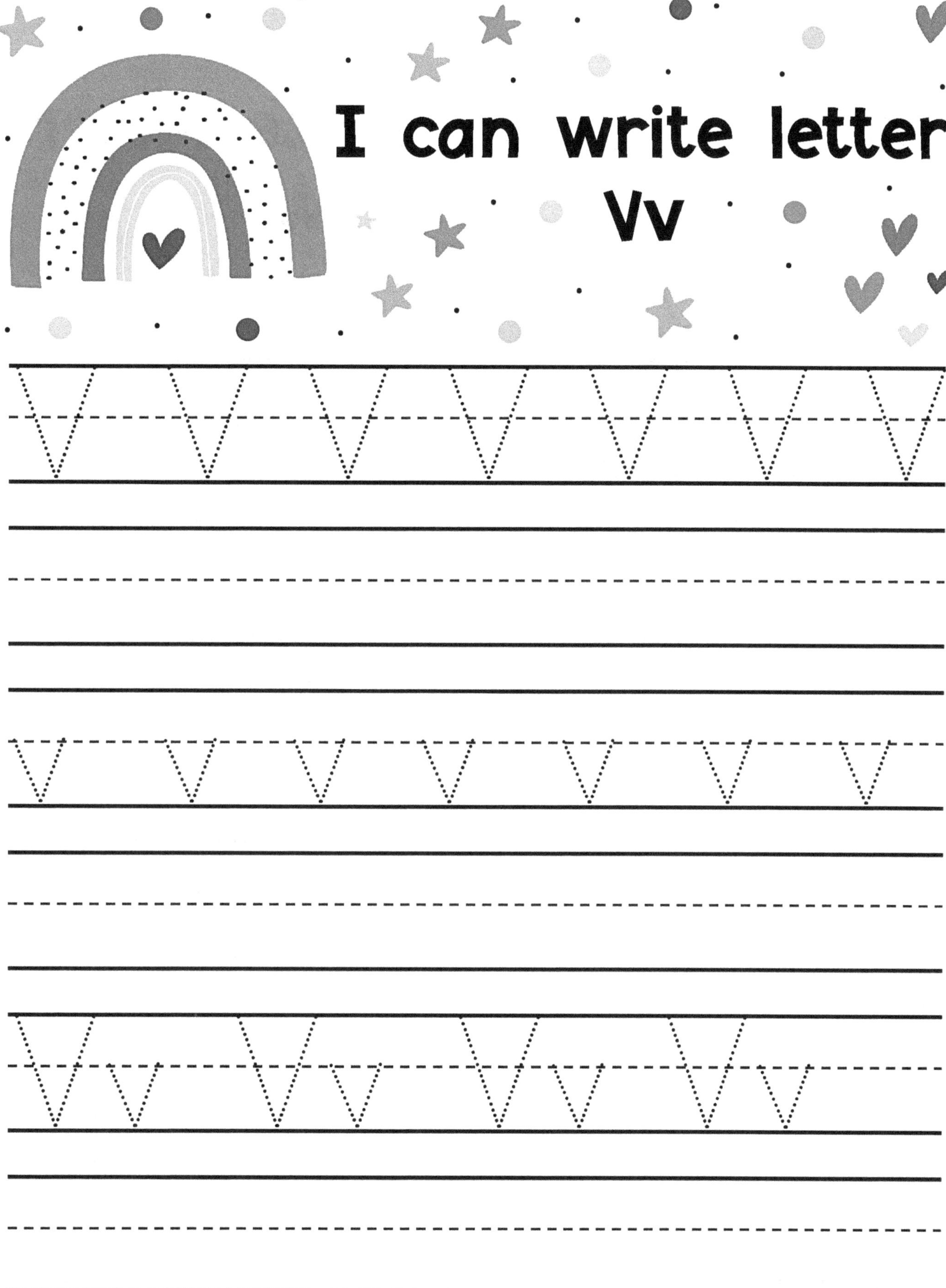

I can write letter Ww

I can write letter Xx

I can write letter Yy

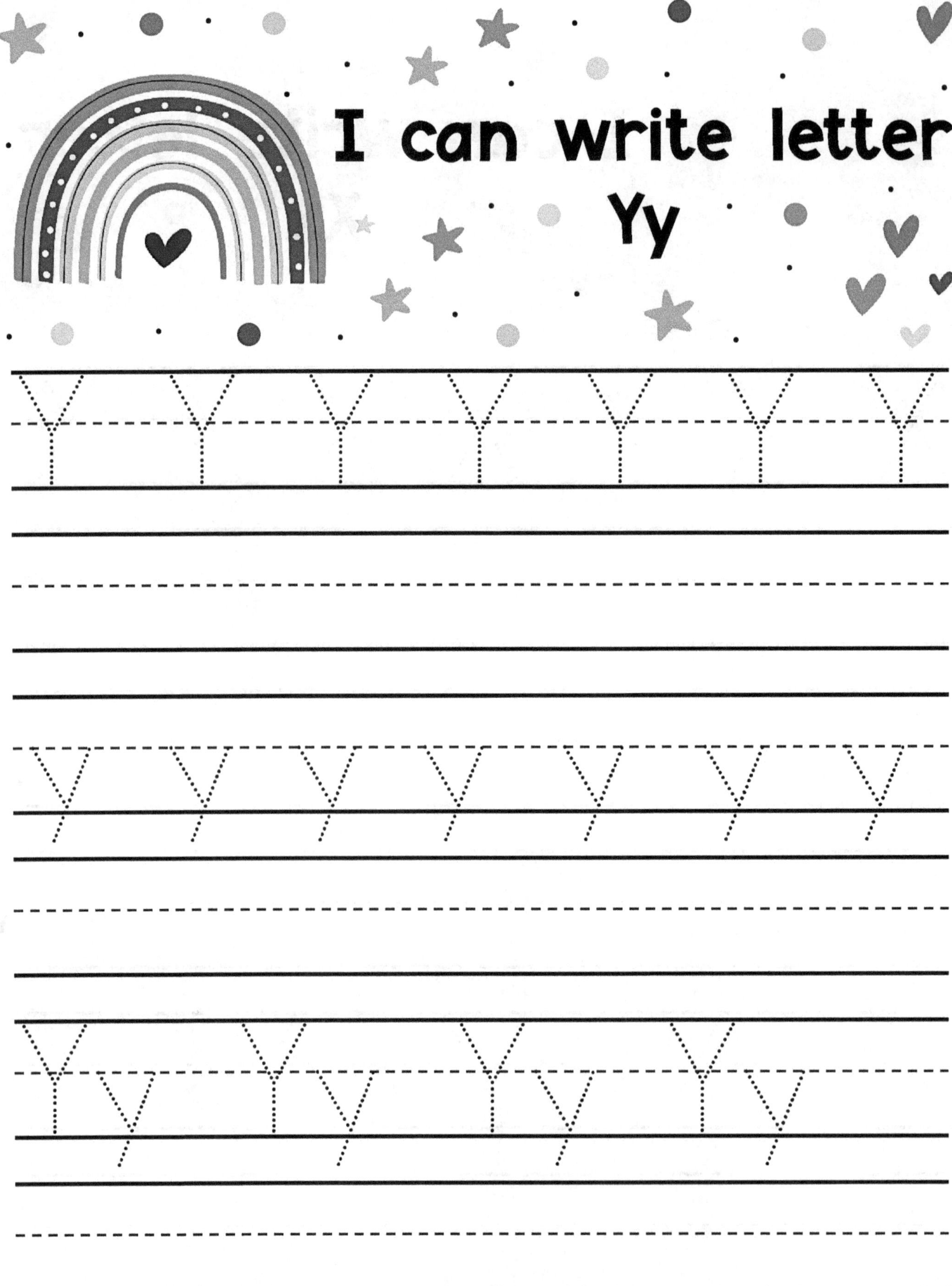

I can write letter Zz

Thank you

**We hope you enjoyed our book
As a small family company,
your feedback is very
important to us.
Please let us know
how you like our
book at :
PROMOBILEAMZ@GMAIL.COM**

Daytona Thorson

CPSIA information can be obtained
at www.ICGtesting.com
Printed in the USA
LVHW010350260121
677405LV00008B/171